TENNIS
Journal

NAME _____

SEASON YEAR _____

CLUB NAME _____

My Tennis Journal

©The Life Graduate Publishing Group

No part of this book may be scanned, reproduced or distributed in any printed or electronic form without the prior permission of the author or publisher.

My Tennis Journal

-Tennis -

My Tennis Journal

-Tennis -

TENNIS Journal SECTIONS

01 Season Goals

Write down your Top 3 Season Goals

02 Training & Game Logbook

Record your training sessions and game details

03 Season Notes

Write further details of your season to keep a record for future reference

04 Autographs & Photos

Gather the autographs and photos of other players, coaches and famous players

01
SEASON GOALS

01 TENNIS SEASON GOALS

GOAL 1 ....
....
....

GOAL 2 ....
....
....

GOAL 3 ....
....
....

My Tennis Journal

- Tennis -

02

TRAINING & GAME LOGBOOK

TRAINING

Date: /   /   Start time   :

                          End time   :

Skills Completed
Write down the skills you worked on and developed during your training sessions

....
....
....
....

Skills to improve
Write down areas that you can improve on for your next training session

....
....
....
....

Coach & Team Focus
Write down if your coach or team has a skill or game focus you are working on

....
....

Extra Notes
Do you have additional notes or thoughts you would like to write down?

....
....
....

GAME DAY

Date: /   /   Start time   :

Location: ....

Home Game   Away Game

Game Details

.... Vs ....

Game Result

Coach Feedback

....
....
....

My Performance   Write down how you felt you contributed to the game. Did the coach provide you any personal feedback? Did you have any highlights? Did you have areas of improvement?

....
....
....
....
....
....

TRAINING

Date: / /　　　　**Start time**　　:

　　　　　　　　　　　　End time　　　:

Skills Completed　　Write down the skills you worked on and developed during your training sessions

....
....
....
....

Skills to improve　　Write down areas that you can improve on for your next training session

....
....
....
....

Coach & Team Focus　　Write down if your coach or team has a skill or game focus you are working on

....
....

Extra Notes　　Do you have additional notes or thoughts you would like to write down?

....
....
....

GAME DAY

Date: /   /   **Start time**   :

Location: ....

Home Game ⚪   **Away Game** ⚪

Game Details

.... **Vs** ....

Game Result

Coach Feedback

....
....
....

My Performance   Write down how you felt you contributed to the game. Did the coach provide you any personal feedback? Did you have any highlights? Did you have areas of improvement?

....
....
....
....
....

TRAINING

Date: / /   **Start time** :

End time :

Skills Completed
Write down the skills you worked on and developed during your training sessions

....
....
....
....

Skills to improve
Write down areas that you can improve on for your next training session

....
....
....
....

Coach & Team Focus
Write down if your coach or team has a skill or game focus you are working on

....
....

Extra Notes
Do you have additional notes or thoughts you would like to write down?

....
....
....

GAME DAY

Date: /   /   Start time   :

Location: ....

Home Game ○   Away Game ○

Game Details

.... Vs ....

Game Result

Coach Feedback

....
....
....

My Performance
Write down how you felt you contributed to the game. Did the coach provide you any personal feedback? Did you have any highlights? Did you have areas of improvement?

....
....
....
....
....

TRAINING

Date: / /   **Start time** :

End time :

Skills Completed   Write down the skills you worked on and developed during your training sessions

....
....
....
....

Skills to improve   Write down areas that you can improve on for your next training session

....
....
....
....

Coach & Team Focus   Write down if your coach or team has a skill or game focus you are working on

....
....

Extra Notes   Do you have additional notes or thoughts you would like to write down?

....
....
....

GAME DAY

Date: / /   **Start time** :

Location: ....

Home Game   **Away Game**

Game Details

.... **Vs** ....

Game Result

Coach Feedback

....
....
....

My Performance
Write down how you felt you contributed to the game. Did the coach provide you any personal feedback? Did you have any highlights? Did you have areas of improvement?

....
....
....
....
....

TRAINING

Date: / / **Start time** :

End time :

Skills Completed
Write down the skills you worked on and developed during your training sessions

....
....
....
....

Skills to improve
Write down areas that you can improve on for your next training session

....
....
....
....

Coach & Team Focus
Write down if your coach or team has a skill or game focus you are working on

....
....

Extra Notes
Do you have additional notes or thoughts you would like to write down?

....
....
....

GAME DAY

Date: / /   Start time   :

Location: ....

Home Game ⚪   Away Game ⚪

Game Details

.... Vs ....

Game Result

Coach Feedback

....
....
....

My Performance

Write down how you felt you contributed to the game. Did the coach provide you any personal feedback? Did you have any highlights? Did you have areas of improvement?

....
....
....
....
....

TRAINING

Date: / /   **Start time** :

End time :

Skills Completed Write down the skills you worked on and developed during your training sessions

....
....
....
....

Skills to improve Write down areas that you can improve on for your next training session

....
....
....
....

Coach & Team Focus Write down if your coach or team has a skill or game focus you are working on

....
....

Extra Notes Do you have additional notes or thoughts you would like to write down?

....
....
....

GAME DAY

Date: / /   **Start time**   :

Location: ....

Home Game ◯   **Away Game** ◯

Game Details

.... **Vs** ....

Game Result

Coach Feedback

....
....
....

My Performance Write down how you felt you contributed to the game. Did the coach provide you any personal feedback? Did you have any highlights? Did you have areas of improvement?

....
....
....
....
....

TRAINING

Date: / /   **Start time** :

End time :

Skills Completed
Write down the skills you worked on and developed during your training sessions

....
....
....
....

Skills to improve
Write down areas that you can improve on for your next training session

....
....
....
....

Coach & Team Focus
Write down if your coach or team has a skill or game focus you are working on

....
....

Extra Notes
Do you have additional notes or thoughts you would like to write down?

....
....
....

GAME DAY

Date: /   /   Start time   :

Location: ....

Home Game ⚪   Away Game ⚪

Game Details

.... Vs ....

Game Result

Coach Feedback

....
....
....

My Performance
Write down how you felt you contributed to the game. Did the coach provide you any personal feedback? Did you have any highlights? Did you have areas of improvement?

....
....
....
....
....
....

TRAINING

Date: / /   **Start time** :

End time :

Skills Completed Write down the skills you worked on and developed during your training sessions

....
....
....
....

Skills to improve Write down areas that you can improve on for your next training session

....
....
....
....

Coach & Team Focus Write down if your coach or team has a skill or game focus you are working on

....
....

Extra Notes Do you have additional notes or thoughts you would like to write down?

....
....
....

GAME DAY

Date: / /   **Start time**   :

Location: ....

Home Game   **Away Game**

Game Details

.... **Vs** ....

Game Result

Coach Feedback

....
....
....

My Performance Write down how you felt you contributed to the game. Did the coach provide you any personal feedback? Did you have any highlights? Did you have areas of improvement?

....
....
....
....
....

TRAINING

Date: / /   Start time :

End time :

Skills Completed
Write down the skills you worked on and developed during your training sessions

....
....
....
....

Skills to improve
Write down areas that you can improve on for your next training session

....
....
....
....

Coach & Team Focus
Write down if your coach or team has a skill or game focus you are working on

....
....

Extra Notes
Do you have additional notes or thoughts you would like to write down?

....
....
....

GAME DAY

Date: /   /   Start time   :

Location: ....

Home Game   Away Game

Game Details

.... Vs ....

Game Result

Coach Feedback

....
....
....

My Performance

Write down how you felt you contributed to the game. Did the coach provide you any personal feedback? Did you have any highlights? Did you have areas of improvement?

....
....
....
....
....
....

TRAINING

Date: / /

Start time :

End time :

Skills Completed
Write down the skills you worked on and developed during your training sessions

....
....
....
....

Skills to improve
Write down areas that you can improve on for your next training session

....
....
....
....

Coach & Team Focus
Write down if your coach or team has a skill or game focus you are working on

....
....

Extra Notes
Do you have additional notes or thoughts you would like to write down?

....
....
....

GAME DAY

Date: /   /   Start time   :

Location: ....

Home Game ⚪   Away Game ⚪

Game Details

.... Vs ....

Game Result

Coach Feedback

....
....
....

My Performance

Write down how you felt you contributed to the game. Did the coach provide you any personal feedback? Did you have any highlights? Did you have areas of improvement?

....
....
....
....
....

TRAINING

Date: / / **Start time** :

End time :

Skills Completed
Write down the skills you worked on and developed during your training sessions

....
....
....
....

Skills to improve
Write down areas that you can improve on for your next training session

....
....
....
....

Coach & Team Focus
Write down if your coach or team has a skill or game focus you are working on

....
....

Extra Notes
Do you have additional notes or thoughts you would like to write down?

....
....
....

GAME DAY

Date: /   /   Start time   :

Location: ....

Home Game   **Away Game**

Game Details

.... Vs ....

Game Result

Coach Feedback

....
....
....

My Performance
Write down how you felt you contributed to the game. Did the coach provide you any personal feedback? Did you have any highlights? Did you have areas of improvement?

....
....
....
....
....
....

TRAINING

Date: /   /   **Start time**   :

End time   :

Skills Completed   Write down the skills you worked on and developed during your training sessions

....
....
....
....

Skills to improve   Write down areas that you can improve on for your next training session

....
....
....
....

Coach & Team Focus   Write down if your coach or team has a skill or game focus you are working on

....
....

Extra Notes   Do you have additional notes or thoughts you would like to write down?

....
....
....

GAME DAY

Date: /   /   Start time   :

Location: ....

Home Game   Away Game

Game Details

.... Vs ....

Game Result

Coach Feedback

....
....
....

My Performance — Write down how you felt you contributed to the game. Did the coach provide you any personal feedback? Did you have any highlights? Did you have areas of improvement?

....
....
....
....
....

TRAINING

Date: / /   **Start time** :

End time :

Skills Completed   Write down the skills you worked on and developed during your training sessions

....
....
....
....

Skills to improve   Write down areas that you can improve on for your next training session

....
....
....
....

Coach & Team Focus   Write down if your coach or team has a skill or game focus you are working on

....
....

Extra Notes   Do you have additional notes or thoughts you would like to write down?

....
....
....

GAME DAY

Date: / /   Start time   :

Location: ....

Home Game   Away Game

Game Details

.... Vs ....

Game Result

Coach Feedback

....
....
....

My Performance

Write down how you felt you contributed to the game. Did the coach provide you any personal feedback? Did you have any highlights? Did you have areas of improvement?

....
....
....
....
....

TRAINING

Date: / /   **Start time** :

End time :

Skills Completed   Write down the skills you worked on and developed during your training sessions

....
....
....
....

Skills to improve   Write down areas that you can improve on for your next training session

....
....
....
....

Coach & Team Focus   Write down if your coach or team has a skill or game focus you are working on

....
....

Extra Notes   Do you have additional notes or thoughts you would like to write down?

....
....
....

GAME DAY

Date: / /   **Start time** :

Location: ....

Home Game   **Away Game**

Game Details

.... **Vs** ....

Game Result

Coach Feedback

....
....
....

My Performance — Write down how you felt you contributed to the game. Did the coach provide you any personal feedback? Did you have any highlights? Did you have areas of improvement?

....
....
....
....
....

TRAINING

Date: / /

Start time :

End time :

Skills Completed
Write down the skills you worked on and developed during your training sessions

....
....
....
....

Skills to improve
Write down areas that you can improve on for your next training session

....
....
....
....

Coach & Team Focus
Write down if your coach or team has a skill or game focus you are working on

....
....

Extra Notes
Do you have additional notes or thoughts you would like to write down?

....
....
....

GAME DAY

Date: /   /   Start time   :

Location: ....

Home Game ⚪   Away Game ⚪

Game Details

.... Vs ....

Game Result

Coach Feedback

....
....
....

My Performance

Write down how you felt you contributed to the game. Did the coach provide you any personal feedback? Did you have any highlights? Did you have areas of improvement?

....
....
....
....
....

TRAINING

Date: / / **Start time** :

End time :

Skills Completed   Write down the skills you worked on and developed during your training sessions

....
....
....
....

Skills to improve   Write down areas that you can improve on for your next training session

....
....
....
....

Coach & Team Focus   Write down if your coach or team has a skill or game focus you are working on

....
....

Extra Notes   Do you have additional notes or thoughts you would like to write down?

....
....
....

GAME DAY

Date: /   /   Start time   :

Location: ....

Home Game ○   Away Game ○

Game Details

.... Vs ....

Game Result

Coach Feedback

....
....
....

My Performance — Write down how you felt you contributed to the game. Did the coach provide you any personal feedback? Did you have any highlights? Did you have areas of improvement?

....
....
....
....
....
....

TRAINING

Date: / / **Start time** :

End time :

Skills Completed Write down the skills you worked on and developed during your training sessions

....
....
....
....

Skills to improve Write down areas that you can improve on for your next training session

....
....
....
....

Coach & Team Focus Write down if your coach or team has a skill or game focus you are working on

....
....

Extra Notes Do you have additional notes or thoughts you would like to write down?

....
....
....

GAME DAY

Date: /   /   Start time   :

Location: ....

Home Game ⚪   Away Game ⚪

Game Details

.... Vs ....

Game Result

Coach Feedback

....
....
....

My Performance   Write down how you felt you contributed to the game. Did the coach provide you any personal feedback? Did you have any highlights? Did you have areas of improvement?

....
....
....
....
....

TRAINING

Date: /   /   **Start time**   :

End time   :

Skills Completed   Write down the skills you worked on and developed during your training sessions

....
....
....
....

Skills to improve   Write down areas that you can improve on for your next training session

....
....
....
....

Coach & Team Focus   Write down if your coach or team has a skill or game focus you are working on

....
....

Extra Notes   Do you have additional notes or thoughts you would like to write down?

....
....
....

GAME DAY

Date: /   /   Start time   :

Location: ....

Home Game ⚪   Away Game ⚪

Game Details

.... Vs ....

Game Result

Coach Feedback

....
....
....

My Performance

Write down how you felt you contributed to the game. Did the coach provide you any personal feedback? Did you have any highlights? Did you have areas of improvement?

....
....
....
....
....

TRAINING

Date: / /   **Start time** :

End time :

Skills Completed   Write down the skills you worked on and developed during your training sessions

....
....
....
....

Skills to improve   Write down areas that you can improve on for your next training session

....
....
....
....

Coach & Team Focus   Write down if your coach or team has a skill or game focus you are working on

....
....

Extra Notes   Do you have additional notes or thoughts you would like to write down?

....
....
....

GAME DAY

Date: /   /   Start time   :

Location: ....

Home Game ⚪   Away Game ⚪

Game Details

.... Vs ....

Game Result

Coach Feedback

....
....
....

My Performance

Write down how you felt you contributed to the game. Did the coach provide you any personal feedback? Did you have any highlights? Did you have areas of improvement?

....
....
....
....
....
....

TRAINING

Date: / /   **Start time** :

End time :

Skills Completed   Write down the skills you worked on and developed during your training sessions

....
....
....
....

Skills to improve   Write down areas that you can improve on for your next training session

....
....
....
....

Coach & Team Focus   Write down if your coach or team has a skill or game focus you are working on

....
....

Extra Notes   Do you have additional notes or thoughts you would like to write down?

....
....
....

GAME DAY

Date: / / **Start time** :

Location: ....

Home Game   **Away Game**

Game Details

.... **Vs** ....

Game Result

....
....
....

Coach Feedback

....
....
....

My Performance   Write down how you felt you contributed to the game. Did the coach provide you any personal feedback? Did you have any highlights? Did you have areas of improvement?

....
....
....
....
....

TRAINING

Date: / /   **Start time** :

End time :

Skills Completed — Write down the skills you worked on and developed during your training sessions

....
....
....
....

Skills to improve — Write down areas that you can improve on for your next training session

....
....
....
....

Coach & Team Focus — Write down if your coach or team has a skill or game focus you are working on

....
....

Extra Notes — Do you have additional notes or thoughts you would like to write down?

....
....
....

GAME DAY

Date: /   /   Start time   :

Location: ....

Home Game ○   Away Game ○

Game Details

.... Vs ....

Game Result

Coach Feedback

....
....
....

My Performance — Write down how you felt you contributed to the game. Did the coach provide you any personal feedback? Did you have any highlights? Did you have areas of improvement?

....
....
....
....
....

TRAINING

Date: / / **Start time** :

End time :

Skills Completed Write down the skills you worked on and developed during your training sessions

....
....
....
....

Skills to improve Write down areas that you can improve on for your next training session

....
....
....
....

Coach & Team Focus Write down if your coach or team has a skill or game focus you are working on

....
....

Extra Notes Do you have additional notes or thoughts you would like to write down?

....
....
....

GAME DAY

Date: /   /   Start time   :

Location: ....

Home Game ○   Away Game ○

Game Details

.... Vs ....

Game Result

Coach Feedback

....
....
....

My Performance — Write down how you felt you contributed to the game. Did the coach provide you any personal feedback? Did you have any highlights? Did you have areas of improvement?

....
....
....
....
....

TRAINING

Date: / /   **Start time**   :

End time   :

Skills Completed
Write down the skills you worked on and developed during your training sessions

....
....
....
....

Skills to improve
Write down areas that you can improve on for your next training session

....
....
....
....

Coach & Team Focus
Write down if your coach or team has a skill or game focus you are working on

....
....

Extra Notes
Do you have additional notes or thoughts you would like to write down?

....
....
....

GAME DAY

Date: / /   Start time :

Location: ....

Home Game ○   Away Game ○

Game Details

.... Vs ....

Game Result

Coach Feedback

....
....
....

My Performance Write down how you felt you contributed to the game. Did the coach provide you any personal feedback? Did you have any highlights? Did you have areas of improvement?

....
....
....
....
....
....

TRAINING

Date: / /   **Start time** :

End time :

Skills Completed
Write down the skills you worked on and developed during your training sessions

....
....
....
....

Skills to improve
Write down areas that you can improve on for your next training session

....
....
....
....

Coach & Team Focus
Write down if your coach or team has a skill or game focus you are working on

....
....

Extra Notes
Do you have additional notes or thoughts you would like to write down?

....
....
....

GAME DAY

Date: /   /   **Start time**   :

Location: ....

Home Game ⚪   **Away Game** ⚪

Game Details

.... **Vs** ....

Game Result

Coach Feedback

....
....
....

My Performance

Write down how you felt you contributed to the game. Did the coach provide you any personal feedback? Did you have any highlights? Did you have areas of improvement?

....
....
....
....
....

TRAINING

Date: / /   **Start time** :

End time :

Skills Completed Write down the skills you worked on and developed during your training sessions

....
....
....
....

Skills to improve Write down areas that you can improve on for your next training session

....
....
....
....

Coach & Team Focus Write down if your coach or team has a skill or game focus you are working on

....
....

Extra Notes Do you have additional notes or thoughts you would like to write down?

....
....
....

GAME DAY

Date: / / Start time :

Location: ....

Home Game   **Away Game**

Game Details

.... **Vs** ....

Game Result

Coach Feedback

....
....
....

My Performance

Write down how you felt you contributed to the game. Did the coach provide you any personal feedback? Did you have any highlights? Did you have areas of improvement?

....
....
....
....
....
....

TRAINING

Date: / / **Start time** :

End time :

Skills Completed — Write down the skills you worked on and developed during your training sessions

....

....

....

....

Skills to improve — Write down areas that you can improve on for your next training session

....

....

....

....

Coach & Team Focus — Write down if your coach or team has a skill or game focus you are working on

....

....

Extra Notes — Do you have additional notes or thoughts you would like to write down?

....

....

....

GAME DAY

Date: / /   **Start time**   :

Location: ....

Home Game ◯   **Away Game** ◯

Game Details

.... **Vs** ....

Game Result

―――――――――――――――――――――

Coach Feedback

....
....
....

My Performance   Write down how you felt you contributed to the game. Did the coach provide you any personal feedback? Did you have any highlights? Did you have areas of improvement?

....
....
....
....
....

TRAINING

Date: / / **Start time** :

End time :

Skills Completed — Write down the skills you worked on and developed during your training sessions

....
....
....
....

Skills to improve — Write down areas that you can improve on for your next training session

....
....
....
....

Coach & Team Focus — Write down if your coach or team has a skill or game focus you are working on

....
....

Extra Notes — Do you have additional notes or thoughts you would like to write down?

....
....
....

GAME DAY

Date: /   /   Start time   :

Location: ....

Home Game   Away Game

Game Details

.... Vs ....

Game Result

Coach Feedback

....
....
....

My Performance

Write down how you felt you contributed to the game. Did the coach provide you any personal feedback? Did you have any highlights? Did you have areas of improvement?

....
....
....
....
....

TRAINING

Date: / /   **Start time** :

End time :

Skills Completed
Write down the skills you worked on and developed during your training sessions

....
....
....
....

Skills to improve
Write down areas that you can improve on for your next training session

....
....
....
....

Coach & Team Focus
Write down if your coach or team has a skill or game focus you are working on

....
....

Extra Notes
Do you have additional notes or thoughts you would like to write down?

....
....
....

GAME DAY

Date: /   /   Start time   :

Location: ....

Home Game ○   Away Game ○

Game Details

.... Vs ....

Game Result

Coach Feedback

....
....
....

My Performance — Write down how you felt you contributed to the game. Did the coach provide you any personal feedback? Did you have any highlights? Did you have areas of improvement?

....
....
....
....
....

TRAINING

Date: / / **Start time** :

End time :

Skills Completed — Write down the skills you worked on and developed during your training sessions

....
....
....
....

Skills to improve — Write down areas that you can improve on for your next training session

....
....
....
....

Coach & Team Focus — Write down if your coach or team has a skill or game focus you are working on

....
....

Extra Notes — Do you have additional notes or thoughts you would like to write down?

....
....
....

GAME DAY

Date: /   /   Start time   :

Location: ....

Home Game ⚪   **Away Game** ⚪

Game Details

.... Vs ....

Game Result

Coach Feedback

....
....
....

My Performance

Write down how you felt you contributed to the game. Did the coach provide you any personal feedback? Did you have any highlights? Did you have areas of improvement?

....
....
....
....
....

TRAINING

Date: / / **Start time** :

End time :

Skills Completed
Write down the skills you worked on and developed during your training sessions

....
....
....
....

Skills to improve
Write down areas that you can improve on for your next training session

....
....
....
....

Coach & Team Focus
Write down if your coach or team has a skill or game focus you are working on

....
....

Extra Notes
Do you have additional notes or thoughts you would like to write down?

....
....
....

GAME DAY

Date: / / **Start time** :

Location: ....

Home Game ⬤ **Away Game** ⬤

Game Details

.... **Vs** ....

Game Result

Coach Feedback

....
....
....

My Performance Write down how you felt you contributed to the game. Did the coach provide you any personal feedback? Did you have any highlights? Did you have areas of improvement?

....
....
....
....
....

TRAINING

Date: / /

Start time :

End time :

Skills Completed
Write down the skills you worked on and developed during your training sessions

....
....
....
....

Skills to improve
Write down areas that you can improve on for your next training session

....
....
....
....

Coach & Team Focus
Write down if your coach or team has a skill or game focus you are working on

....
....

Extra Notes
Do you have additional notes or thoughts you would like to write down?

....
....
....

GAME DAY

Date: /   /   Start time   :

Location: ....

Home Game ○   **Away Game** ○

Game Details

.... **Vs** ....

Game Result

Coach Feedback

....
....
....

My Performance
Write down how you felt you contributed to the game. Did the coach provide you any personal feedback? Did you have any highlights? Did you have areas of improvement?

....
....
....
....
....
....

TRAINING

Date: / / **Start time** :

End time :

Skills Completed
Write down the skills you worked on and developed during your training sessions

....
....
....
....

Skills to improve
Write down areas that you can improve on for your next training session

....
....
....
....

Coach & Team Focus
Write down if your coach or team has a skill or game focus you are working on

....
....

Extra Notes
Do you have additional notes or thoughts you would like to write down?

....
....
....

GAME DAY

Date: /   /   Start time   :

Location: ....

Home Game   **Away Game**

Game Details

.... **Vs** ....

Game Result

Coach Feedback

....
....
....

My Performance   Write down how you felt you contributed to the game. Did the coach provide you any personal feedback? Did you have any highlights? Did you have areas of improvement?

....
....
....
....
....

My Tennis Journal

- Tennis -

03

SEASON NOTES

NOTES

NOTES

NOTES

NOTES

My Tennis Journal

-Tennis-

04

Autographs & Photos

Autographs & Photo's

Autographs & Photo's

Autographs & Photo's

Autographs & Photo's

TENNIS
Journal

-Tennis-

www.ingramcontent.com/pod-product-compliance
Lightning Source LLC
Chambersburg PA
CBHW080325151125
35492CB00017B/1808